WEEK

Edinburgh

ILLUSTRATED BY
Lucy Davey

pocket mountains

With thanks to my parents, Tony and Elizabeth, for instilling a love of walking in me.

Published by
Pocket Mountains Ltd
The Old Church, Annanside,
Moffat DG10 9HB

ISBN: 978-1-907025-60-0

Printed in Poland

Introduction

Edinburgh is one of the most richly layered and picturesque historical cities in the world. From the New Town's neoclassical ensembles and their grand façades to the pre-Reformation architecture of the Old Town, it has been Scotland's capital for almost 600 years and attracts visitors from across the world, all year round.

Together, the Old Town spilling down the ridge of the Royal Mile with its medieval 'fishbone' street pattern and its organic architectural eclecticism and, on the plain below, the New Town, the finest example of Georgian town planning in Europe, form a UNESCO World Heritage Site.

New Town and Old Town join hands in 'the great arena' of Sir Walter Scott's Waverley Valley, and for many visitors their first glimpse of the city is from Waverley, a meeting point overlooked by what is probably the largest monument to a writer anywhere in the world.

Few could sum up Edinburgh's character better than Scott's contemporary, Lord Henry Cockburn, when he wrote in 1849 of 'our curious and matchless position, our strange irregularity of surface' and 'its picturesque results' – created by the

Firth of Forth to the north and the Pentland Hills to the south, the dramatic topography of the Old Town and the purposeful alignment of buildings in both Old and New Towns.

Like Rome, Edinburgh has its Seven Hills. Formed from an extinct volcano complex in the heart of the city, Castle Rock, Arthur's Seat and Calton Hill offer a sweeping overview of the urban skyline and its most famous landmarks, as well as being an inextricable part of that skyscape, forming – in the words of Lord Cockburn – 'the endless aspect of the city, as looked down from adjoining heights, or as it presents itself to the plains below'.

Offering more distant perspectives over the city are the Craiglockhart Hills and Corstorphine Hill, while Blackford Hill and the Braid Hills are the most remote of the Seven. Other lofty vantage points include the slopes above Swanston in the Pentland Hills, lauded both by Lord Cockburn and Robert Louis Stevenson.

Landmarks that you will see from near and far on these walks include Edinburgh Castle issuing from its rock, the bright confusion of pointy roofs,

turrets and chimney stacks of Ramsay Garden, the Bank of Scotland prevailing over the New Town from its perch on the Mound, the spire of St Giles', the Greek Revival monuments across the valley on Calton Hill and, down below, the Old Royal High School, the Scott Monument, the galleries in Princes Street Gardens and the Melville Monument soaring from the redesigned centre of St Andrew Square.

There is a hidden Edinburgh, too. Obscured by a leafy canopy, the Water of Leith, Edinburgh's 'silver thread in a ribbon of green' which once powered 70 or 80 mills, slips unseen past some of the northern New Town's finest classical streets before emptying into the Firth of Forth at the regenerated Port of Leith. Behind the solid wall of the Pentland Hills are little glens that seem so remote it's hard to believe they lie on the doorstep of a seat of power. Over to the north, many coastal gems also lie concealed – South Queensferry cowering in the shadow of another UNESCO World Heritage Site, the Forth Bridge, the old milling village of

Cramond, the former fishing harbour at Musselburgh and the nature reserves and beaches of East Lothian.

As you walk these routes, you will find reminders that great historical figures have been this way before, including Scotland's most celebrated royal, Mary, Queen of Scots, at the Palace of Holyroodhouse, at Carberry Hill, at Seton and at Roslin, while there are numerous associations with one or other of Edinburgh's most famous literary sons, Sir Walter Scott and Robert Louis Stevenson – at South Queensferry, Corstorphine Hill, Bonaly, Swanston, Colinton and at Roslin too.

It is impossible, of course, to explore Edinburgh on foot without reference to the Scottish Enlightenment, the period of intellectual, literary, scientific and artistic achievement, which reached its zenith in the decades either side of the 1770s, with a rollcall of leading lights that included Robert Burns, Robert Fergusson, David Hume, Adam Smith, Adam Ferguson, James Boswell, James Hutton, Allan Ramsay and Henry Raeburn present at almost every turn. The most influential architect of the era, Robert Adam, designed Charlotte Square, the pinnacle of New Town planning, but he also had a hand in Seton Castle, Gosford House and structures at Dalkeith Palace; while W H Playfair designed many of the city's finest neoclassical edifices.

To admire the most central of these highlights, you'll find a choice of trains, buses and trams while, further out, many routes can be reached by public transport with a little effort – check in advance at www.travelinescotland.com. Be aware that exploring sites beyond the city streets involves responsibilities for the walker. This includes keeping dogs on leads near livestock, sticking to paths to avoid disturbing habitats or grouse-shooting activities, showing consideration near private residences and observing diversions, common near water or in forestry.

On some of the shorter routes a map is not necessary, but an Ordnance Survey (OS) map can be invaluable on longer or hill routes, as well as the ability to use one with a compass: the sketch maps in the book are intended to provide rough guidance only.

Edinburgh: Weekend Walks

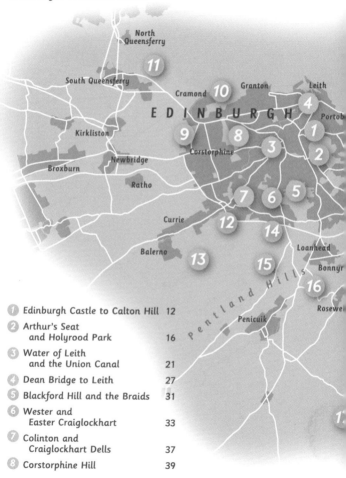

North Queensferry

South Queensferry

Cramond

Granton

Leith

Portob

EDINBURGH

Kirkliston

Corstorphine

Newbridge

Broxburn

Ratho

Currie

Balerno

Loanhead

Bonnyr

Pentland Hills

Rosewe

Penicuik

Contents

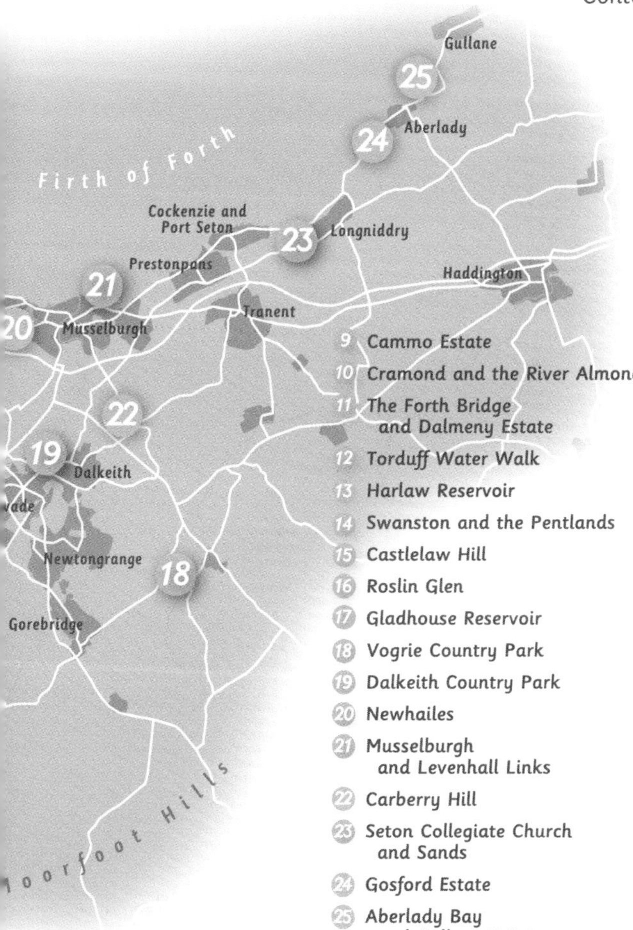

Map labels:
Gullane
Aberlady
Firth of Forth
Cockenzie and Port Seton
Longniddry
Prestonpans
Haddington
Tranent
Musselburgh
Dalkeith
Newtongrange
Gorebridge
Moorfoot Hills

1

Edinburgh Castle to Calton Hill

Distance **3.5km** Time **2 hours (at least)**
Terrain **pavements** Access **trains, trams and buses to Waverley Stn**

This walk ventures into the heart of the Old Town while casting an eye over the fringes of the Georgian New Town from two of the city centre's most iconic hills.

Begin at Waverley Station, named after Sir Walter Scott's popular early 19th-century series of novels, in the very centre of the city. Leave by the Market Street exit, turning right to follow the road to a roundabout at the top of Waverley Bridge.

On your right is a gate to Princes Street Gardens, created in the 1820s from the fetid Nor' Loch and linking the Old and New Towns; the gothic spire of the Scott Monument is on the far side. Scott, who had a key to the once private gardens, admired them greatly on his walk from his New Town home to his work at the courts on the Royal Mile.

Continuing above the gardens and beneath the looming 1806 Bank of Scotland building, you emerge at the top of the Mound, formed from the tons of earth and rubble removed in the 1780s to make way for the New Town. (If you wish, you can detour through the gardens to visit the neoclassical National Gallery of Scotland and the Royal Scottish Academy; rejoin the route up the steep Playfair Steps, named after the galleries' designer W H Playfair, credited with transforming Georgian Edinburgh into a modern 'Athens of the North'.)

Cross the road to head up past Edinburgh University's 1846 New College onto Ramsay Lane, passing the curious Ramsay Garden, to reach Castlehill at the top of the Royal Mile. Unless you arrive before breakfast you may be caught in the surge of visitors to the castle to the right, its vast esplanade looking out over the city.

From here, plunge straight down the Royal Mile's granite setts, between the jumble of towering tenements bisected by a warren of narrow closes within

which so much of the Old Town's historic life was conducted. Some are open to the public: Lady Stair's Close, on the Lawnmarket, where national bard Robert Burns stayed on his first visit to the capital, houses a small Writers' Museum dedicated to Burns, Scott and R L Stevenson. Opposite this Fisher's Close leads to an elevated look-out over Victoria Street with the capital's most photogenic row of shops, while just up from Lady Stair's, James Court was home to diarist James Boswell, and to philosopher David Hume – whose statue sits outside the High Court further down, a reminder that many Scottish Enlightenment figures were also legal scholars, advocates and judges.

Opposite the High Court, a memorial to one of the Old Town's shadier characters, Deacon Brodie, sits in the form of an eponymous tavern. Town councillor and cabinetmaker by day and burglar by night, Brodie is said to have inspired Stevenson's *The Strange Case of Dr Jekyll and Mr Hyde*. Further down by St Giles' Cathedral is the place where Brodie was hanged in 1788 on the gallows which, popular legend has it, he had helped to design. Forty years later, another infamous execution took place near here, that of William Burke who, with William Hare, committed a series of grisly murders in order to sell the cadavers to the university's anatomy classes. A crowd of 25,000 turned out for his execution.

St Giles' is set within Parliament

Square, where Parliament House was used by the Scottish parliament until the Union with England in 1707. Thronged with street performers during the August Fringe Festival, and tourists at any time, you may have trouble locating the Heart of Midlothian, a pattern of stones that marks the entrance to the Old Tolbooth, used as a prison until its demolition in 1817.

At Cockburn Street, turn left, or cut down through dingy Anchor Close, known for the howff once frequented by the Crochallan Fencibles, a drinking club whose members included William Smellie, founder of the *Encyclopaedia Brittanica* and publisher of Burns. Drop down Cockburn Street to the roundabout and go straight on over Waverley Bridge and up to Princes Street. Opposite the Scott Monument, South St David Street leads to St Andrew Square, once the prestigious financial heart of the city. 'St David' is said to jokingly refer to Hume, a committed atheist, who lived his last years here. This route leads right, however, above Waverley Station and past the Balmoral (once the North British) Hotel to go straight on at a junction, up Waterloo Place. After 200m pass Old Calton Burial Ground, final resting place of Hume, who in the 18th century successfully campaigned for a public walkway on Calton Hill.

To reach the hilltop, cross the road by St Andrew's House, one of Scotland's most important art deco buildings. Go up steps, turning right at another set to emerge at the collection of historic structures, some designed by Playfair, including the National Monument, an incomplete replica of the Parthenon to commemorate those who died in the Napoleonic Wars; City Observatory, in the style of a Greek temple; and the circular Greek Revival monument to philosopher Dugald Stewart.

The view from Calton Hill sweeps over the landmarks passed on the walk – the soaring tower of St Giles', the Florentine-style dome of the Bank of Scotland, the castle rising out of its rock, the Scott Monument – and across the Firth of Forth to the Ochil Hills. Return down the hill and past the Balmoral Hotel to Waverley Station.

2

Arthur's Seat and Holyrood Park

Distance **3.5km** Time **2 hours 30**
Terrain **surfaced and unsurfaced paths and tracks, steps and rocky ground** Map **OS Explorer 350** Access **buses to the foot of the Royal Mile, near Holyrood Park**

If you like your hills populated by visitors from all corners of the world with superb views and a big dose of history thrown in then head to the bottom of the Royal Mile and begin the walk up Arthur's Seat.

For drivers, the route starts at the car park beside the Palace of Holyroodhouse, but there are a few approaches on foot from the city centre. One of the best crosses Waverley Bridge, then climbs Cockburn Street, built to provide carriage from the Old Town to Waverley Station in 1856 and named after Lord Henry Cockburn. From here, go straight down the Royal Mile to its end, passing the medieval John Knox House (the leader of the Reformation in Scotland was minister at St Giles' from 1559, though it is doubtful he ever actually lived here in this house).

The adjacent Moubray House was occupied for a time by Daniel Defoe, author of *Robinson Crusoe*, who was sent to the capital as a propagandist and spy for the English government in the uneasy run-up to the 1707 Union.

Cross St Mary's Street to reach the Canongate. This marks the site of the Flodden Wall, built to protect the 10,000 residents within its increasingly crowded confines from a potential English invasion following the Scots' defeat at the 1513 Battle of Flodden with England. (A detour right takes you to a preserved stretch of the wall.)

Pass the iconic turreted steeple and clock of the Old Tolbooth, originating from 1591 when the Canongate was distinct from the Royal Burgh of Edinburgh. Behind this stretch of the Royal Mile are the secretive Dunbar's

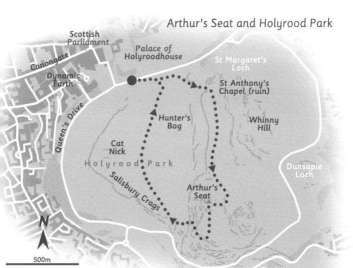

Close garden; Panmure Close, once home to Adam Smith, author of *The Wealth of Nations*; and Old Playhouse Close which led to the first post-Reformation theatre built in the city, shut down by the church in 1786.

At the foot of the Canongate, the road sweeps to the right around the Scottish Parliament building. Completed in 2004, its windows recall the famous *Skating Minister*, a painting attributed to Scottish Enlightenment-era artist Henry Raeburn.

Pass the entrance to the Renaissance-style Palace of Holyroodhouse, the Royal family's official residence in Scotland. It was here that David Rizzio, secretary of Mary, Queen of Scots, was murdered in 1566, while in 1745 a 60,000-strong crowd greeted Bonnie Prince Charlie on the Royal Mile as he arrived to hold court here. The origins of Edinburgh's renowned Royal Botanic Garden also lie within the Palace grounds in the 1670 Physic Garden – before it was moved to a site now occupied by Waverley Station's Platform 11.

Cross the road from the car park

and go left on a surfaced path parallel to the road (not the footpath next to it). As the path begins to bend right, go left along an unsurfaced trail. Ignore turnings and continue to widely-spaced steps which lead up to the right. Over to the left are the ruins of St Anthony's Chapel. Though little is recorded of its origins, it is thought to have been linked to nearby Holyrood Abbey and that the Pope paid for repairs in the 15th century.

Follow the main path as it swings right and ignore turnings to the left. You then aim straight for the top of Arthur's Seat before bearing left below it. On reaching a level section of ground with views over the Firth of Forth, go right to follow a path by a metal chain fence. This leads steeply up to the top and its breathtaking views. Over to the south is Duddingston Loch, the only natural freshwater loch in Edinburgh where, in the 18th century, the Reverend Robert Walker of Canongate Kirk, long accepted as the subject of Raeburn's much-loved painting, skated.

Beyond the viewfinder, follow a path round to the left. Thread your way carefully down rocks to a wide grassy area. With the summit behind you, head towards the top of this, then take a path just to its left.

The path drops steeply and swings round to the right before a series of zigzags with stone steps leads further down. At the bottom, turn right and follow a path down below a grassy hillside which leads to the top of the curved sill of Salisbury Crags, where in 1788 Edinburgh scientist and philosopher James Hutton based the theories that now underpin the modern study of geology. Below the crags is the Radical Road, whose creation was led by Sir Walter Scott to give work to local unemployed weavers in the 19th century.

The return path continues all the way to the start, but first take a detour up the hillside to the top of Salisbury Crags with its views over the Palace, the roofline of the Scottish Parliament building – designed to recall these very crags – and Thomas Hamilton's 1829 neoclassical Old Royal High School, feted as Scotland's finest example of Greek Revival architecture, below Calton Hill.

3

Water of Leith and the Union Canal

Distance **10.5km** Time **3 hours 30**
Terrain **unsurfaced and surfaced paths, steps, pavements**
Map **OS Explorer 350**
Access **trains, trams and buses to Haymarket Station**

Explore hidden Edinburgh by following its network of paths and tracks along old railway lines, riverbanks and canal towpaths and across parkland.

Start at the main entrance to Haymarket Station, which lies just beyond Edinburgh's West End. If you are arriving from Princes Street, the neoclassical arcs of Coates and Atholl Crescents are an elegant distraction from the trams and buses that ply the main thoroughfare. Behind Coates Crescent lies the centrepiece of the Western New Town – the broad sweep of Melville Street's Georgian terraces – and, tucked between the two, the more intimate scale of William Street's parade of independent shopfronts and eateries with accommodation for artisans and tradesmen. All three streets were designed by the same architect, Robert Brown, in the early 1800s. The gothic spires of St Mary's Cathedral dominate the west end of Melville Street where notable past residents include, at Melville Crescent, Dr Joseph Bell, an eminent surgeon who would achieve lasting fame as the inspiration for the world's most famous fictional detective, Arthur Conan Doyle's Sherlock Holmes.

From the station entrance, go left to follow the tramlines which then drop left. At the bottom of the hill, keep parallel with the tracks: a path continues where the road leaves off and, where it meets a residents' car park, heads around the block of housing to continue by the tramlines and soon join Balbirnie Place. Follow this road downhill, crossing at a blue cycleway sign to continue on the Roseburn Path. After a short distance, go right via the blue sign for

Queensferry, keep left at the next junction and cross the A8 on an old bridge which carried the Granton branch of the Caledonian Railway until the 1960s.

After 200m go left down a steep fight of steps to the Water of Leith Walkway, where you turn left and follow the river upstream. A short flight of steps soon leads onto Roseburn Cliff. The row of cottage villas at the top of this road were part of a social experiment conceived by Patrick Geddes, botanist, biologist and the father of modern town planning, echoing his best known project, Ramsay Garden, on Castlehill – but the scheme was not fully realised. Turn right to walk down to and cross Roseburn Terrace to the right, then go down Roseburn Gardens to the bottom, turning right here.

Head right again around the edge of Roseburn Park – Murrayfield Rugby Stadium is on the other side – to Murrayfield Ice Rink. Take a path to the right of the car park entrance to rejoin the Water of Leith: ignore the

bridge here and the next one but take the one after that to continue upstream on the other side.

After heading beneath tram and train bridges, keep left as you pass but don't cross a wooden footbridge. Beyond the bowling greens you emerge at Balgreen Road, which you cross and follow very

briefly left before turning right to enter Saughton Park. Go left to take a wide surfaced path which begins at the end of a small car park. As it swings round to the right, it passes the restored walled garden with glasshouses and a bandstand. Eventually leaving the park, turn right onto Ford's Road, then left after 20m to follow a footpath to the A71 (Gorgie Road): cross this to continue on the Water of Leith Walkway, crossing the river and passing allotments and a cemetery before going under the 1848 viaduct at Slateford. Running parallel with this is the Slateford Aqueduct, built 25 years earlier to carry the Union Canal, a contour canal for importing coal and lime into Edinburgh. The new railway superseded the canal and within a century the Edinburgh basins were closed. Go left up the steps just before the aqueduct and turn left at the top to join the canal towpath for a delightful green stretch, later passing the red-roofed Ashley Terrace Boathouse, base of the Edinburgh Canal Society, then

Harrison Park on the left and Polwath Parish Church on the right as you head in towards the tenements that crowd above the final 3.5km stretch to the canal basin.

Passing the quayside bars, head to the main Fountainbridge road and cross this to follow Gardner's Crescent. An outlier of Edinburgh's New Town, the crescent comprises typical four-storey tenements but the bid for classical symmetry with an identical crescent opposite was never achieved. Instead, behind the gardens that were to occupy the centre of the circus is the striking brick Rosemount Buildings with its polychrome façade and corner towers. Completed in 1860, this was one of the capital's first industrial housing schemes to break with the tradition of stone building. Just after this you pass the Rosebank Cottages, the first in three rows of early Colony houses built at around the same time as Rosemount Buildings for working people. At a junction with traffic lights, go left to follow Morrison Street for 500m to Haymarket Station.

4

Dean Bridge to Leith

Distance **6.5km** Time **2 hours 15 (one way)** Terrain **surfaced and unsurfaced paths and tracks, pavements** Map **OS Explorer 350** Access **buses and trams to West End Princes Street; return by bus**

Set in a gorge below the Thomas Telford-designed Dean Bridge is picturesque Dean Village, once home to eleven mills. On this walk, the Water of Leith threads its way through here and the former milling village of Stockbridge to wash up at Leith's vibrant waterfront.

For a glimpse of the quiet harmony of the West New Town streets that lie hidden behind the busier classical grid of James Craig's original New Town, start at the west end of Princes Street opposite the red sandstone Caledonian Hotel. This was built above the former Princes Street Station and completed in 1903 as a challenge to Waverley Station's North British Hotel, opened a year earlier. From here walk down Hope Street to Charlotte Square.

Designed by Robert Adam in 1791, Charlotte Square, with its leafy private gardens, is regarded as one of Europe's finest architectural set pieces and the high point of the original New Town. Pass West Register House with its elegant dome modelled on St Paul's Cathedral, and continue down to the circus of Ainslie Place, built in 1822 as part of the western extension of the First New Town and still one of its most prestigious addresses; a left turn will take you up to Randolph Crescent. Both contain private landscaped gardens. Carry on to Queensferry Street and turn right.

Just before Dean Bridge, go down Bell's Brae to Dean Village. Turn left down Hawthornbank Lane for a view of the tenements of Well Court, built in the 1880s as model housing for millworkers. Cross the footbridge to Damside, ignoring the Water of Leith Walkway sign for the Dean Gallery and Scottish National Gallery of Modern Art; instead turn right around Well Court to a junction. On the left at the top of a hill is Edinburgh's own necropolis – Dean Cemetery – the final resting place of Sir John Murray, founder of modern oceanography, W H Playfair, Lord Henry Cockburn, Lord Francis Jeffrey and the Nasmyths. However, this route turns right to cross Bell's Bridge and follow Miller Row on the left.

The Water of Leith Walkway leads on from here, passing far below Dean Bridge to St Bernard's Well where a natural spring was discovered in the 18th century; Alexander Nasmyth designed the ornate pump room with its statue of Hygeia, Greek

goddess of health. Continue on a lower walkway to pass beneath a stone bridge and along a road to Stockbridge. Cross the main road ahead and then the bridge (left) towards this former mill village's main street, Raeburn Place, named after the portrait painter Henry Raeburn who owned much of this land in the 1790s. Go down the steps by the clocktower to rejoin the Water of Leith.

At a bridge leave the river and go

left for 20m before turning right onto Arboretum Avenue (a path also runs between road and river). As you continue, look across the river and you will glimpse the Stockbridge Colonies, a series of model terraces of artisan houses that represented a social improvement experiment in the latter half of the 19th century.

The route joins the Rocheid Path after a metal gate, but if you wish to detour to the Royal Botanic Garden, continue to Arboretum Avenue's end, crossing the main road to follow Arboretum Place to the garden's West Gate on the right. Entry is free to the 70 acres of landscaped garden, though there is a charge for entering the glasshouses, home to more than 3000 exotic plants. Retrace your steps to the metal gate.

Back on the Rocheid Path, cross the second footbridge and carry on downstream. After going under a bridge, climb the steps and turn left to reach the main road by the bridge at Canonmills. Cross the road and go right, then left down Warriston Road. After passing below a stone bridge

the road follows the river to St Mark's Bridge. On the other side, turn right by the water. Ignore two footbridges, then go under a bridge and past a weir before the river sweeps right. Ignore all paths on the left to join the former Edinburgh, Leith and Newhaven Railway Line, passing the old Bonnington Station before rejoining the river. This leads you into Leith where you cross the water at Sandport Place.

Leith has seen something of a transformation since Irvine Welsh set his seminal 1993 novel, *Trainspotting*, here, and the Shore is home to upmarket bars and eateries. Go left and follow it to the Victoria Swing Bridge where you recross the water and turn left to head upstream to a bar. Cross a small bridge and walk over the setts of Dock Place to Commercial Street, where you go left, passing the oldest custom house in Scotland, built in 1810 in neoclassical style. The bus for the city centre stops just before a bridge, or go right to return along the Water of Leith.

Blackford Hill and the Braids

Distance **9km** Time **3 hours 45**
Terrain **surfaced and unsurfaced
paths** Map **OS Explorer 350**
Access **bus from the city centre to
Braidburn Tce, 200m from the start**

**A wander through the ancient
woods of the Hermitage of Braid
gorge and a bracing climb to
Blackford's Royal Observatory is
topped by a sweeping overview
from the main Braid Hills range.**

Start at the signed access track for
Hermitage of Braid, off Braid Road.
Just before a bridge, leave the track
for a path on the left which follows the
burn past an ornate doocot, built in
1788 to keep the newly completed
Hermitage House supplied with pigeon
meat. Cross a small car park at a brick
building to rejoin the main access
track, going right at a fork before the
house, and cross three bridges; ignore
a fourth to go up steps on the left.

The main path takes you left to the
edge of a field. Just after a gate on the
left, go up a dirt path on the right to
climb a long flight of steps. Pass a
telecoms mast on the exposed top and
loop left to Blackford Hill's summit.
The hill's value as a lookout was
recognised by Edward I in 1295 and
Oliver Cromwell in 1650 who both
surveyed the city from camps here.

In Sir Walter Scott's 1808 poem,
Marmion, the hero remembers his
'broomy' boyhood hilltop where the
'murmur of the city crowd' and 'Saint
Giles's mingling din' rose on 'breezes
thin'. A century later and Scott's
Blackford Hill was unrecognisable:
work began in 1896 on an Italianate-
style Royal Observatory to replace
Calton Hill's as a public monument to
astronomy with a state-of-the-art
research centre and one of the world's
greatest astronomical book collections.

Head east from the trig point,
bear right 50m before the observatory
and turn left onto a surfaced track.
Cross a car park, exiting on the right to
head to a bench. Take the same line

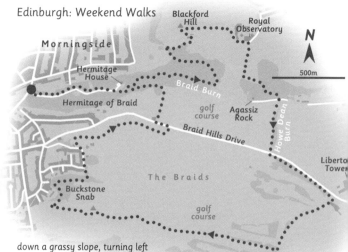

Edinburgh: Weekend Walks

down a grassy slope, turning left before a metal fence. A grass path leads through broom and over another path to reach a wood. Turn right onto a path, weaving down to a track, which you cross.

You can detour right here to Agassiz Rock, named after Louis Agassiz, 'the father of glaciology', who made important discoveries here. After crossing the track follow the Howe Dean Burn path (signed) – bear briefly right, then left, uphill. Ignore all turnings to meet Braid Hill Drive.

Over the road, go through a gate and turn left along a path, turning right at the end onto a track by a golf course. After 500m the track turns right to summit the Braid Hills. From the trig point (beyond two telecoms masts), go down a path which turns right, then left through gorse to the back of houses. Go right, taking a path on the left at the last house. Follow a road to Braid Hills Golf Course, turning left onto a path just through the gates.

After 850m, go left down to Braid Hills Drive again; cross and turn left to take the Lang Linn Path on the right down to a T-junction. Go left here and right at a fork to rejoin the Braid Burn path. Go left to retrace your steps.

Wester and Easter Craiglockhart

Distance 4.5km **Time** 1 hour 45
Terrain surfaced and unsurfaced
paths, pavement, steps **Map** OS
Explorer 350 **Access** buses from
Edinburgh to Colinton Road

**In 1917 the poets Wilfred Owen
and Siegfried Sassoon first met
at Craiglockhart War Hospital,
established to help shell-shocked
officers returning from the First
World War. The 1877 Italianate
building, now part of Napier
University, sits below one of the
city's Seven Hills.**

It was here, in this beautiful former
hydropathic institute, that Owen wrote
one of his best-known poems, *Dulce et
Decorum Est*, before returning to the
trenches where he was killed just days
before the Armistice. Though, like its
slightly lower neighbour Easter
Craiglockhart, the hill sits amidst golf
courses and housing, its mix of open
grassland and woods makes it a haven
for plants and wildlife, with a sea of flag

iris and forget-me-nots, as well as
many less common flowering plants and
grasses, in spring and early summer.

Start from the bottom of Lockharton
Crescent, a short walk from Colinton
Road if arriving by bus. Go through
a gap in the railings, signed for
Craiglockharton Hills Conservation
Area, and follow a sett-laid path to a
junction. Turn right, ignore steps to the
left and skirt along Craiglockhart
Pond, used in Victorian times for
curling and skating, and now a habitat
for birdlife – mute swans have nested
here for more than a century. Continue
behind a sports centre and, as the
path climbs uphill, go straight on at a
junction, ignoring a path on the left.

Emerging at Glenlockhart Road, the
former war hospital is to the right while
the route follows the pavement left for
100m. Cross the road to go through a
gate on the other side, then turn left
onto a woodland path. This is the most
direct route up Wester Craiglockhart
Hill and avoids a golf course.

Craiglockhart

Colinton Road

Easter
Craiglockhart
Hill

Glenlockhart Road

Craiglockhart
Hydropathic

Wester
Craiglockhart
Hill

N

500m

The path goes right as it gains
height; at a track go sharp right to
follow an earth and grass path. At a
junction go left to follow the hill's
ridge to its top and trig point. With
sweeping views across the capital, it is
easy to see why this hilltop was
chosen as the site for a fort from 2AD.

Retrace your steps to the road and
along the path on the other side. At the
first junction go right, up steps and
through woodland. At another junction
go right, down steps and through a
gap in a wall. Ignore a well-built path
going left and take a grassy path up to
the right to reach the top of Easter
Craiglockhart Hill with views back to
the first hill of the day.

Keep a fence to your right as you
cross the hilltop, turning left once
through a gap in a wall. A path drops
down to the edge of the grounds of
Craig House, where you go left to pass
an information board and leave the
woods. At the bottom of widely
spaced steps go right, down a grassy
meadow (the turning is just before the
gap in the wall passed earlier). The
path enters woods and descends steps
– ignore the first gap in a wall but go
through the second before turning
sharp left.

A path leads behind houses to go
down a short flight of steps on the
left. Shortly after, go right to follow
the path with the setts back to
Lockharton Crescent and the start.

7

Colinton and Craiglockhart Dells

Distance 4km Time **1 hour 30**
Terrain **surfaced and unsurfaced
paths, steps** Map **OS Explorer 350**
Access **buses from Edinburgh to
the Water of Leith Visitor Centre**

**The Water of Leith is described
as a 'silver thread in a ribbon of
green' and nowhere is this more
apparent than on this sylvan
stretch through the gorge of the
Colinton and Craiglockhart Dells.**

More than 70 mills once clung to the
banks of the river with the tidal mouth
a focus for whaling and shipbuilding,
as well as sugar refining and brewing
nearby, earning it the ignominious title
by 1889 of the most polluted stream in
Scotland. With signs of industry long
gone, the riverside is returning to nature.

From the Water of Leith Visitor
Centre at Slateford, cross the busy
A70 and turn left, then take the path
on the right just before a converted
stone cottage to enter the Dells.

At a fork, drop right to stay by the

river and reach an old grotto, built in
the 18th century for visitors to surgeon
Dr Alexander Monro's Craiglockhart
Estate and originally decorated with
shells. Beyond this, cross a small
footbridge and, ignoring a bridge over
the Water of Leith, go right at a
junction to drop down steps and
continue by the river. You may spy
kingfisher, heron or dippers here, as
well as roe deer on the wooded slopes.

Cross the stone Bogs Mill Bridge and
continue upstream on an undulating
path, keeping left at a junction to
cross back over the river and carry on
past a house to reach a stone cottage
at the bottom of a minor road. Turn
right to follow the wide path (with
fence) and then go down steps to the
lade for Redhall Mill. Cross a bridge
with views to Redhall's impressive
weir just upstream. The mill produced
paper for banknotes from 1718 before
being converted into a barley mill.

Continue upstream to reach Colinton
Village, an 'Arcadia' for R L Stevenson

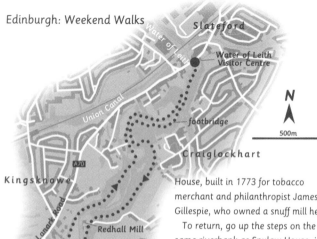

who spent what he described as his 'Golden Age' here while his grandfather was minister of the parish kirk. Past the kirk and a seated statue of the author, cross the river and go up Spylaw Street, turning right between the gateposts after the pub to drop to the river, crossing it beneath the B701 roadbridge to see the splendid Spylaw House, built in 1773 for tobacco merchant and philanthropist James Gillespie, who owned a snuff mill here.

To return, go up the steps on the same riverbank as Spylaw House, just before the roadbridge. Turn right to join the Water of Leith Walkway and go through a well-lit railway tunnel decorated with stunningly colourful and creative murals. At a signpost go straight on, taking the second right after 700m, then almost immediate left back to the river.

Pass Bogs Mill Bridge again (don't cross) and stay on the riverside path, keeping right at a junction to shadow the river. After going down a short flight of steps, the path leads past the 18th-century Redhall Walled Garden. When you reach the first footbridge passed on the walk, cross and turn left to retrace your steps to the start.

1/04/23

8

Corstorphine Hill

Distance **4km** Time **1 hour 45**
Terrain **surfaced and unsurfaced
paths, some steps**
Map **OS Explorer 350** Access **buses
from Edinburgh and the Gyle
Centre to Clermiston Road North**

**A maze of hill paths take you
high above Edinburgh, far
removed from the suburbs that
spill out from the West End.
Once at the top, views open up
across the city. Stay alert, as
you may hear, or even glimpse,
some of the zoo's exotic
residents as you pass behind it.**

Start 500m south of Queensferry
Road on Clermiston Road North where
there is a bus stop and small car park.
Take the track beside the car park,
soon turning right onto a path that
leads up into woodland.

Ignore paths on both sides as you
gain height, then after a wooden
barrier keep left to descend slightly
before continuing gently uphill. Ignore
steps to the right and carry on ahead
as, further on, steps join from the left.

At the next junction (by a stone
marker) go straight on, then keep left.

At the edge of a golf course a
sweeping view opens out across the
capital. The path steepens and
narrows as it bears right here. At a
junction, go left to follow the high
metal boundary of Edinburgh Zoo.
One of its most famous former
residents was Wotjek, the Soldier Bear
(whose memorial can be seen in West
Princes Street Gardens). Beloved in
Poland, Wotjek was adopted by Polish
soldiers in the Second World War, was
on the frontline in the Battle of Monte
Cassino, and was enlisted as an
honorary soldier and mascot in 1944.

You soon reach the board and bench
at the Rest and Be Thankful viewpoint,
so named as it offered weary
travellers their first stunning outlook
of the city. Here, Davie Balfour and
Alan Breck Stewart part company as
they look 'down on Corstorphine
bogs and over to the city and the
castle' in R L Stevenson's novel
Kidnapped. Walk a bit further on for
views to the Pentland Hills.

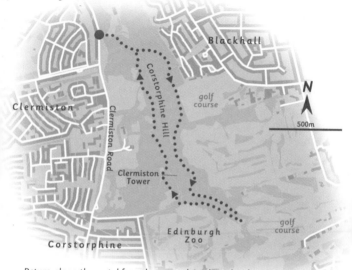

Return along the metal fence but don't follow your earlier path to the right; instead continue over the south side of the hill. Ignore a short flight of steps to the left and go straight on here and at the bottom of some steps. At a junction, go right uphill to cross a grassy area and reach a marker post in the woods. Turning right here, you come to Clermiston Tower, built in 1871 to mark the centenary of Sir Walter Scott's birth. Beyond, the path makes a twisting descent to the left before resuming its course along the broad north ridge. Go straight ahead at a junction, then bear slightly right to go up some smooth rock slabs. Bear left just before the top of these to cross more rocks and drop down to the left.

After 50m go left to leave the woods and drop down to a large field, where you go right at a bench. Cross the top corner of the field to a path which takes you straight on into the woods. This leads to another trail, where you turn left to retrace your steps, going right at the fork to return to the start.

9

Cammo Estate

Distance **2.5km** Time **1 hour 15**
Terrain **surfaced and unsurfaced
paths** Map **OS Explorer 350**
Access **buses from Edinburgh stop
near the Cammo Road junction on
Queensferry Road**

**Cammo Estate was once one of
the most desirable addresses in
Edinburgh. The main house was
built for wealthy landowner
John Menzies in 1693, but the
changing fortunes and growing
eccentricities of later occupants
led to its demise and the rise in
claims that it may have inspired
the ominous unfinished 'barrack'
of the House of Shaws in Robert
Louis Stevenson's *Kidnapped.***

Cammo is now a glorious ruin slowly
being reclaimed by nature but
retaining some of its former grandeur,
as are the walled garden and stable
block passed on this walk. Unlike some
former stately homes this is not a
place overburdened with information
boards. The walk proper begins at the
estate entrance at the bottom of
Cammo Road. (If driving here,
continue to the car park at the end
of Cammo Walk. From there you can
follow the path round to the right to
the start point.) Walk past the large
iron gates at Cammo Lodge and
onto an old driveway. This leads up
and to the right to reach the remains
of the house itself. After exploring,
go to the far side of the ruins and
take a path which begins on the
right of a large redwood – part of
a pinetum established during the
estate's heyday.

After passing beneath an old beech
tree to reach a clearing, go left at a
junction of paths, then left again at
the next junction to pass the end of
the estate's ornamental canal. At the
following junction go right and walk
along the edge of the estate until just
before a field, where you go left.

As the path veers right there is a
wonderful example of nature
reasserting itself as you cross a small
meadow and pass through a gap in a
wall. The entrance to an old walled
garden is on the left but the route

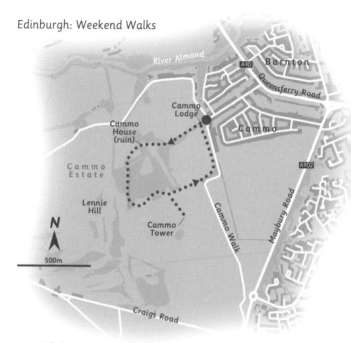

goes right here, along a surfaced path. This leads to the former stable block which is well worth peeking around with its ornate stonework. It is slightly less ruined than the main house, which passed to the Watsons of Saughton in 1741 and was eventually taken over by the National Trust for Scotland in 1980.

Take a path on the right of the stable block which leads across a field to Cammo Tower, built in the 19th century as a watertower but now only home to birds. Behind it is a little hill that makes a great picnic spot and vantage point over the estate.

Cross back over the field and go right to head down to the car park. If you arrived by bus, the path on the left side of the car park goes round to the left (don't enter the meadow on the left) to reach Cammo Lodge.

10

Cramond and the River Almond

Distance **8km** Time **2 hours 30**
Terrain **surfaced and unsurfaced
paths, minor roads, steps**
Map **OS Explorer 350** Access **buses
from Edinburgh to Cramond**

**Cramond is a picturesque
village that would not be out
of place on a remote stretch of
coastline yet it lies on the
doorstep of the capital.**

From the bus stop on Cramond Road
North, you can walk down Cramond
Glebe Road, passing Cramond Kirk
under which the principia of a Roman
fort lies partially buried – Cramond's
early life began as a Roman harbour
station for the Antonine Wall from
141AD and was reoccupied by Emperor
Septimus Severus half a century later.
On the right, Kirk Cramond leads to the
partly excavated site and to the private
Cramond Tower, originally designed as
the summer palace of the Bishops of
Dunkeld in the 16th century.

For drivers, the car park is just on

the right before you emerge at the
village foreshore with its whitewashed
houses and little marina, usually
packed with sailing craft in the
warmer months. Before you set out,
detour to the shore of the Firth of
Forth where it is possible to cross the
causeway to Cramond Island: check
tide times on the noticeboard to avoid
becoming stranded.

The walk heads left up the River
Almond and past the Cramond Boat
Club. A sign then indicates the start
of the River Almond Walkway. Keep
right to stay by the river and up a
path which continues at the end of a
road to Fair-a-far weir and the old mill
remains. The weir was originally built
around 1790 as a watersource for the
ironworks established by industrialist
Sir William Cadell. The Cadell
Company employed around 100
workers in four mills along the river,
importing bar iron from Russia and
Sweden. Few traces of the steam
forges, furnaces, engine sheds and

horse-tramways that served the mills remain, and peace is disturbed only by planes coming into land nearby.

The route continues to some steep flights of steps, then goes high above the river before descending more steps. Stay by the water until you reach a minor road. Follow this up to a junction and go right to reach the end of Cramond Old Brig, but don't cross; instead keep left to walk along the edge of a paddock.

At the end of this, go right to walk through trees, jink left, then turn right along a path. Just before the busy A90, go down steps on the

right and follow a riverside path below the road. This rises, then falls, reaching a small wooden bridge over a burn before going up to the left and passing between two garden fences.

At a road go right and once at the top of a bend take a path on the right, immediately after a driveway for '52 Woodley'. The path leads to a stone bridge over the river; cross this and begin the return by the waterside. After passing back below the A90, you emerge at a small car park behind a pub. Cross this and turn right to go over Cramond Old Brig before retracing your steps to the start.

11

The Forth Bridge and Dalmeny Estate

Distance **8km** Time **2 hours**
Terrain **minor roads, drives, tracks and some paths** Map **OS Explorer 350** Access **buses from Edinburgh to Hawes Pier and trains to Dalmeny Station (on the route)**

Begin from one of the greatest feats of Victorian engineering to explore a sandy beach with distant views and a country estate with wood and parkland.

The Forth Bridge is a UNESCO World Heritage Site and people have been admiring it from Hawes Pier in South Queensferry since before construction was finished in 1890. Just behind the snapping cameras is the Hawes Inn, another place steeped in 19th-century history. It is said Robert Louis Stevenson was inspired to write *Kidnapped* while staying in Room 13 in 1886, and one of the key passages – the planning of Davie Balfour's abduction – is set in the hostelry.

The walk begins from the RNLI station opposite the inn. Head under the bridge, then bear left away from the main road and down a track. This leads to Long Craig Gate, a coastal entrance to the Dalmeny Estate. The estate has been the seat of the Earls of Rosebery since the 17th century and walkers are welcome as long as they keep dogs on leads and away from the sheep.

Soon the track leads to Hound Point, said to be haunted by the ghost of a dog owned by Sir Richard Mowbray, who died in the Crusades. Despite the legend and the oil terminal offshore, it is worth lingering; take the path detouring left for views back to the bridges. Behind the Forth Bridge is the Forth Road Bridge, the world's longest suspension bridge when it opened in 1964, and then the 2017 Queensferry Crossing, the world's longest three-tower cable-stayed bridge when built.

This path rejoins the main track on the other side of the point, where Drum Sands make a fine spot to picnic beneath Scots pine and watch for the

49

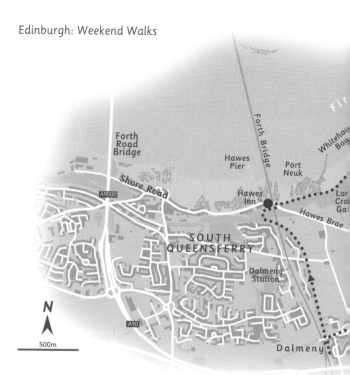

N

500m

many oystercatchers and curlew that feed here. In a while the route passes Barnbougle Castle, a private residence dating back to medieval times but rebuilt in the 19th century. In his short time as Prime Minister, the fifth earl, Archibald Primrose, practised his speeches in the main hall.

Further on is the 'big house', built in 1817. Dalmeny House was designed, unusually for the times, in fanciful Tudor Gothic style by William Wilkins, a university friend of the fourth earl, who was also responsible for the National Gallery in London and much of King's College, Cambridge – parts of which bear some resemblance to Dalmeny.

The drive of the house leads away

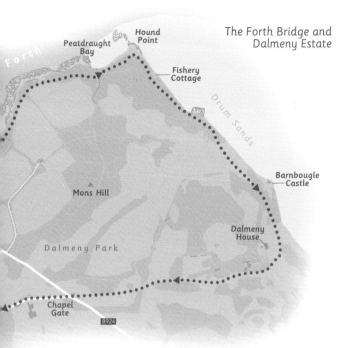

from the shore and goes up to the
right, past a statue of a horse – King
Tom. Instead of continuing by the
coast go slightly left at a junction and
up an estate driveway to reach Chapel
Gate, about 2km from the main house.

Cross the busy main road to a
quieter road on the other side that
takes you to the pretty village of
Dalmeny. Go straight on past the
cottages until the road bends left –

carry straight on here, then turn left,
following a blue sign for 'Queensferry'.

A ramp leads to a path beside the
railway; go right and follow it for 1km
to reach a footbridge just after passing
below the southern end of the Forth
Bridge. A path on the right leads back
round to the right to go under the
railway bridge. At this point follow
steps on the left, down to a road and
go left to return to Hawes Pier.

12

Torduff Water Walk

Distance **2.5km** Time **1 hour 15**
Terrain **unsurfaced and surfaced
paths, minor road**
Map **OS Explorer 350**
Access **buses from Edinburgh to
Bonaly Road, 1km from the start**

**The waymarked Torduff Water
Walk is an easy route around
a small Victorian-era reservoir
in the northern Pentland Hills.
It is best enjoyed in late summer
when the moorland is awash
with purple heather.**

The route starts at a car park at the
very top of Bonaly Road, beyond a
bridge over the city bypass and past
the grounds of Bonaly Tower and the
Bonaly Scout Centre. Now private
apartments, Bonaly Tower was once
home to Edinburgh preservationist and
advocate, later to become Solicitor
General for Scotland, Lord Henry
Cockburn. He was known to host the
'Friday Club' here, members of which
included Francis Jeffrey, founder and
editor of the *Edinburgh Review*, and
Sir Walter Scott. The original 17th-

century farmhouse lay at the heart
of Bonaly village, but the settlement
was cleared after Lord Cockburn's
purchase in 1811. A 'peel tower',
designed by W H Playfair, was added
in 1839 and wings were attached in
1870 and 1888.

From the car park, go through a
gate and continue uphill in the same
direction as the road, following a sign
for the Torduff Water Walk on a stony
path which climbs steeply through
Sanctuary Wood.

At the top of the wood go right
immediately before a gate to follow a
path with heather-clad moorland to
your left and the trees down to the
right. In summer the moor is a mass of
purple heather, one of the highlights of
any walk in the Pentlands. The lucky
white variety may be harder to spot,
but its mythical ability to confer good
fortune on those in possession of it
stems from the works of Ossian, an
Irish warrior-bard dubbed the 'Homer
of the North', who was, in fact, a great
18th-century hoax by Scottish poet
James Macpherson.

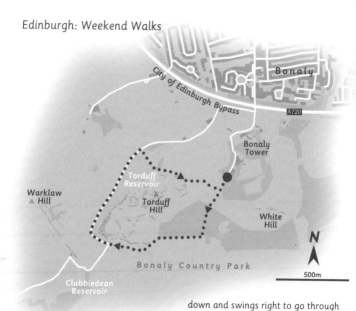

At the end of the wood turn left through a metal gate where a short detour to the right takes you to the base of a pylon with a view sweeping over the edge of the Pentlands to the city skyline, where a number of historic buildings owe their continued existence to the influence of Lord Cockburn on 19th-century attitudes towards architectural conservation. The Firth of Forth can be seen shimmering beyond.

Back at the gate, take the grassy path leading straight ahead: this drops down and swings right to go through another metal gate, then descends steeply through two more gates to reach a minor road, where you go right. A wood and metal bridge crosses the burn at the head of Torduff Reservoir before the road swings right to follow the water to a dam. Cross the dam and take a trail on the other side which swings to the left of the hillside in front of you. The path then drops down to the gate at the top of Bonaly Road which you went through at the start of the walk.

13

Harlaw Reservoir

Distance **5km** Time **1 hour 30**
Terrain **paths and tracks, muddy
in places** Map **OS Explorer 344**
Access **buses from Edinburgh city
centre to Balerno**

**On the western edge of the
Pentland Hills and yet only
a stone's throw from the city
boundaries, Harlaw Reservoir
is popular with visitors, but it's
easy to leave the crowds behind.**

As can be seen from the dam wall
and other buildings, the reservoir
dates back to Victorian times when
it was built for the Edinburgh Water
Company. While no longer delivering
tap water, it is part of a flood
prevention scheme in the city's
southwest and is used to produce
electricity by the community-owned
Harlaw Hydro co-operative. Water
leaving the reservoir is converted
into power which is fed into the
national grid.

Start the walk from the Harlaw
Reservoir car park, about 2km
southeast of the village of Balerno.

Follow the sign for the Harlaw
Woodland Walk from the end of the
car park to arrive after 200m at the
Harlaw House Visitor Centre, built just
after the reservoir was completed in
1848. In summer this former
waterkeeper's cottage can be busy,
especially when the snack bar is open.

Go right to follow a track over
Harlaw Reservoir's dam. The Bavelaw
Burn leaves Harlaw here to join the
Water of Leith at Balerno, where the
walkway that accompanies this river
begins a journey that will take it
through picturesque former milling
villages to the port of Leith.

Pine trees cover much of the next
stretch of the route and a network of
little paths, created by anglers, is fun
for children to explore, though ensure
you keep them away from the water's
edge. Before long you make your way
to the top of the reservoir and the
outflow from Threipmuir Reservoir.

After crossing a metal bridge go left
and follow a track below Threipmuir's
grassy dam, which is not at this point
visible. Follow the sign for Black

Springs at the end of the dam and bear right to take a path threading through trees.

Emerging from the trees, continue by the water's edge, going straight on through gorse rather than crossing a causeway. Across the water is Black Hill, often a patchwork of burned heather between autumn and early spring. Known as muirburn, the controlled burning of old woody heather to expose new shoots has a long history in the Pentlands; it is a food source for grouse and is in use both on upland farms and shooting estates. From here, look out over the fields for lapwings, or peewits, as well as wildfowl in the reeds at this end of the water.

The route goes left at a gate to climb uphill, passing through two more gates at the top. This sparse woodland is favoured by mushroom hunters, but unless you are an expert yourself the fungi are best left alone. After the next gate, a rough track leads left to a signpost; cross a stone stile here to take a path back to the visitor centre.

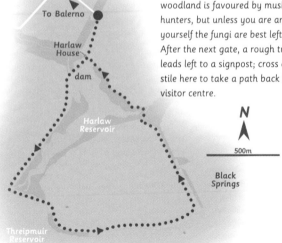

To Balerno

Harlaw House

dam

Harlaw Reservoir

N

500m

Black Springs

Threipmuir Reservoir

14

Swanston and the Pentlands

Distance **4km** Time **1 hour 45**
Terrain **unsurfaced paths, steep in places, tracks, pavement**
Map **OS Explorer 350** Access **buses from Edinburgh to Hillend**

Robert Louis Stevenson, author of *Kidnapped* and *Treasure Island*, spent many summers near the little village of Swanston which lies on the edge of the city in the shadow of the Pentland Hills and is reached after a lovely walk through the foothills of the range.

Little may have changed here since as a young man Stevenson spent holidays striking out into the hills from the nearby villa of Swanston Cottage which the family leased between 1867 and 1880. The white-harled reed-thatched cottages of the village itself are architecturally important for their intact historic fabric and character; they also formed part of the setting for Stevenson's novel *St Ives*.

Signposted as the Capital View Walk, the route starts at the car park at the bottom of the access road for the Midlothian Snowsports Centre (also known as Hillend) – at 450m it has the longest dry ski slope in Europe and can boast that 30 Olympians have trained here.

Follow a path uphill to the left from an information board, bearing left again after 200m on a wide grassy path. Ignoring a path to the left, climb very steeply uphill before going across a junction of paths. A path leads you to the right of a gorse-covered hill before continuing upwards. Here, views open out over the city in which Stevenson found such compelling duality, right down to its 'clashing of architecture' with the 'sacred isles' of the Firth of Forth ranged behind.

After passing between little rocky outcrops, head to the right of a grassy hillock to go through a gate and turn right. A narrow path leads above the ski slopes and then descends – carry on in the same direction at any

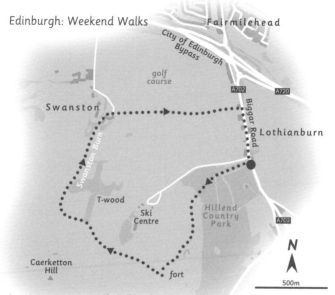

Fairmilehead

City of Edinburgh Bypass

golf course

A702   A720

Swanston

Biggar Road

Lothianburn

Swanston Burn

T-wood

Ski Centre

Hillend Country Park

A703

Caerketton Hill

fort

N

500m

junctions to meet a track. Follow this straight ahead, turning right after the large T-wood on the right: it was planted in the shape of a Greek cross in 1766 by Henry Trotter of Mortonhall in memory of a family member who had fallen in battle.

Keep right to follow the Swanston Burn all the way down to a gate: cattle graze here, so keep dogs on a tight lead. After the gate, follow a track down to an information board on the left. Beyond this, on the left, lies Swanston. The Orcadian poet and

novelist Edwin Muir found his 'little paradise' here while living in Edinburgh in the 1950s, after a deeply traumatic early experience of moving from Orkney to the industrial 'hell' of Glasgow. There is a bench to his memory on the village green.

Pass the thatched roofs and turn right past stone cottages and straight onto a track, signed for Lothianburn, which leads directly to the busy A702. Turn right along the pavement to reach the start after 300m.

15

Castlelaw Hill

Distance **4km** Time **1 hour 30**
Terrain **rough paths and tracks**
Map **OS Explorer 344** Access **buses
from Edinburgh to Easter Howgate,
1.5km from the start**

**At Castlelaw, nestled in the
Pentlands, the history of defence
dates from the Iron Age to the
present day. As a vantage point
it's hard to beat, boasting one
of the best views in all Scotland.**

The Ministry of Defence uses one side
of the hill to test the precision of
servicemen and women with a variety
of weaponry on a shooting range,
while at the foot of Castlelaw lies an
Iron Age hillfort. When red flags are
flying, do not cross into the range.

This route starts at the end of the
signed road off the A702 below the
hillfort. Just to the east of the
turn-off is Crosshouse Farm, where
C T R Wilson was born in 1869: he
received the Nobel Prize for Physics in
1927 for his work on clouds. Go
through a gate at the top of the car
park and follow an obvious track

uphill. This passes the hillfort, which
you can explore. It is thought the site
was home to an Iron Age community
for hundreds of years and, as was
often the case, the Romans used it
after them. As well as the stone
passages, you can still see the
ramparts and to get a sense of their
size it is best viewed from the slopes
above where you can make out three
concentric rings of defences.

Beyond the fort, keep to the main
track as it climbs fairly steeply up and
to the right of Castlelaw Hill. At a
junction much higher up, go left and
follow a track which turns left higher
up and climbs very steeply before
finally reaching the top: the fence
marks the edge of the firing range.

This is a place to linger, particularly
if you arrive as the sun begins to set,
highlighting the bumps and folds of
the hills. To the north are 'topmost
Allermuir' and 'steepest Caerketton'
where in 1890, while living in Samoa,
Robert Louis Stevenson imagined
himself. In the nostalgic poem that
references these hills, 'the Tropics

'vanish' to be replaced by a vision of the two-sided city that inspired his greatest works, with the 'cragged, spired and turreted' form of her 'virgin fort' and the 'seaward-drooping hills' upon which 'new folds of city glitter'.

From this point such city views are blocked by Stevenson's beloved hills – you need to follow the Swanston walk on the far side of Caerketton for these – but in truth this only enhances the feeling of delightful remoteness, with the higher peaks of the Pentland Hills stretching southwards beyond the Thomas Telford-designed Glencorse Reservoir, and Loganlea Reservoir.

The swiftest descent is via a narrow path by the fence to the left, but this is very steep in places and slippery after rain, so return the way you came and enjoy the heather-clad hills without the exertion of the outward route.

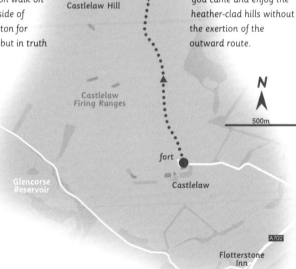

Roslin Glen

Distance **2.5km** Time **1 hour 15**
Terrain **unsurfaced paths (muddy
in places), tracks, minor road**
Map **OS Explorer 344**
Access **buses from Edinburgh to
Roslin, 1km from the start**

**The deep gorge of Roslin Glen
once reverberated to the sound
of gunpowder mills but now
the largest stretch of ancient
woodland in Midlothian is
filled only with birdsong.**

Since Dan Brown set the climax of
his bestselling novel, *The Da Vinci
Code*, at 15th-century Rosslyn Chapel
in 2003, visitor numbers have gone
through the roof, while in recent years
landslips have limited access to the
glen floor, but it is still possible to
enjoy a short dramatic walk filled with
natural and historic wonders.

Start from the Roslin Glen Country
Park car park (signed from the west
end of Roslin village). From the far
side of the car park, cross the grass to
take a path to the right. On meeting
the River North Esk, cross a bridge

and go straight ahead uphill.

Just before some steps turn right to
head beneath an archway, below the
ruins of Rosslyn Castle. The Battle of
Rosslyn, in which a small Scottish
army crushed much larger English
forces, took place near here in 1302
and the earliest remaining parts of the
castle probably date to soon after the
battle. The castle was reduced to its
present state by troops loyal to Oliver
Cromwell in 1650, but it was its
ruinous state and dramatic position
that helped make the glen such a
magnet for writers and artists of
the Romantic period; among those
who sought inspiration here were
J M W Turner, William Wordsworth
and Sir Walter Scott.

Turn left at the bottom of a slope to
follow the river downstream. The path
climbs high above the gorge which is
home to green woodpeckers, buzzards
and kingfishers, as well as badgers
and otters, though you would be very
lucky to see these shy mammals.

Ignore turnings down to the right
until the main path has swung left

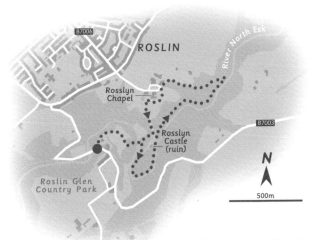

away from the steeper slopes. Then go right in front of a laurel, down a path which leads to a line of yew trees. Turn left here, up a low bank, then left again to almost double back on yourself and reach the start of a path.

Ignore a turning to the right but accompany the main path round to the right and up to a track, where you go left. Here, follow a minor road to the left for 100m before going left at a wooden gate. On the other side turn right to pass behind Rosslyn Chapel. Originally dedicated as the Collegiate Chapel of St Matthew in 1450, it has been the seat of the St Clair family for almost 600 years.

Keep going right, with views to the Pentland Hills. At a driveway, turn right for the chapel (or bus stop) or go down the driveway to continue the route. After a cemetery, go left, between two gates, to follow a track which leads down to the ruins of Rosslyn Castle. Turn right before a bridge to the castle and walk down steps. These take you to the path and bridge over the river, which lead back to the start.

17

Gladhouse Reservoir

Distance **8km** Time **2 hours 30**
Terrain **minor roads, farm tracks,
field edge** Maps **OS Explorer 344
and 345** Access **no regular public
transport to the start**

**Tucked beneath the Moorfoot
Hills near Penicuik is Gladhouse
Reservoir, the largest body of
freshwater in the Lothians.
It is a popular boat-fishing
destination, stocked with brown
trout, as well as being a Site of
Special Scientific Interest which
attracts thousands of pink-
footed geese each winter.**

The route starts at a parking area at
the southwest corner of the reservoir
(GR NT292528). From here, head east
along a minor road to the collection of
houses and a farm which makes up the
settlement of Moorfoot. Go straight
ahead, between barns, to follow a sign
for Huntly Cot, down a track going
left. This swings right and goes up to a
large house at Huntly Cot.

Keep farm buildings to your right,
then follow the track up to the right,

across an open field. Go through a
gate and continue up to a junction of
tracks where you go left at a footpath
sign, through another gate. You are
now high above the reservoir with the
Moorfoot Hills close at hand to the
south while the Lothians are spread
out to the north. In the foreground is
the reservoir, backed by the Pentland
Hills. The reservoir, formerly known as
Moorfoot Loch, was created in 1879 to
meet Edinburgh's growing demand for
water, by engineer James Leslie. For a
time Leslie was articled to William
Playfair, who designed many of
Edinburgh's neoclassical landmarks.

One of the highlights of Gladhouse
Reservoir is its birdlife. Mallard, teal,
tufted duck and great-crested grebe
can all be found here, but it is as a
winter roosting site for pink-footed
geese that it is most significant,
supporting at its peak one-eighth of
the world's population.

Carry straight on to pass to the left
of a small forestry plantation. Go
through a wooden gate and continue
to a fence on the left, beside a field, to

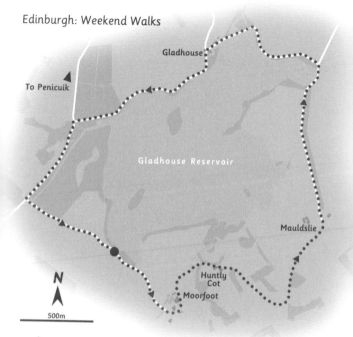

Gladhouse

To Penicuik

Gladhouse Reservoir

Mauldslie

Huntly Cot

Moorfoot

N

500m

reach a gate near Mauldslie Farm.

Go right, down a track, to meet a junction where you go left onto a minor road. After 1km you pass a boatshed on the left before coming to a junction, where you go left. The road follows the reservoir round to its 19th-century dam which you can cross via its grassy path before rejoining the road. After 1.5km go left at a junction to follow another road for a further

750m. Go left again to walk the last 800m back to the start.

Although a lot of this route is on minor roads there is hardly any traffic, meaning the sound you are most likely to hear is that of birdsong – especially lapwings which swoop and circle above the fields in spring. Do also be aware that despite the beauty of the reservoir it is dangerous to swim here, even on a hot sunny day.

18

Vogrie Country Park

Distance **4km** Time **1 hour 45**
Terrain **unsurfaced paths and
tracks, steps** Map **OS Explorer 345**
Access **bus from Edinburgh to
Edgehead Rd, 1.5km from the start**

**The Scottish baronial-style
Vogrie House is set amidst a
designed landscape of gardens
and sweeping carriage drives at
the heart of a woodland estate.
Numerous paths thread their
way through the country park
which also features grassland,
burns and ponds.**

This walk combines two waymarked
trails through the 105 hectares of
woods and Victorian parkland
acquired as a private estate by the
Dewar family in the 18th century. It
has seen various uses since then: as
the Royal Hospital for Nervous
Disorders from 1923 and as a base for
the Civil Defence Force in the Cold
War, before becoming Scotland's
second country park in 1982.

Vogrie is located around 5km from
Gorebridge in Midlothian. Begin the
walk from the car park nearest the
main entrance and head to its left-
hand (north) side to follow a sign for
North Woods Dewarton. When the
path splits keep left to accompany a
road for 100m before re-entering
woodland. Keep left again at a fork
and follow a trail along the north edge
of the country park. Stay on the main
path after crossing a small burn, then
go right at a sign for Vogrie House.

The path swings round to the right
and descends. At a sign for Tyne
Valley, go left along a gorge carrying
the Vogrie Burn. Cross the burn by a
small stone bridge further down and
immediately go left on the other side.
Recross the burn lower down, then go
right to cross the Tyne Water.

A steep path leads uphill to the right,
away from the river, before going
further right and starting to drop
down. After leaving the woodland you
pass a grassy area before turning right
at another sign for Vogrie House to
drop down steps and re-cross the now
rather narrow Tyne Water. Go left,
then right at another junction, again

following a sign for Vogrie House. Go straight on uphill at the next junction, then turn right at a second junction to head beneath huge beech trees. Many of Vogrie's more exotic trees were brought here by George Forrest, one of the country's most prolific plant collectors, who undertook a series of alarming expeditions to Tibet and China's Yunnan Province in the early 20th century, giving rise to his posthumous nickname in more recent times as 'Scotland's Indiana Jones'.

At another junction, go left to emerge on a lawn beside Vogrie House, said to be the finest surviving work of Perth town architect Andrew Heiton, who designed it in 1876 for Lt Col Alexander Cumming Dewar.

Walk left around the building to the front before taking the second path to the left of an information board in front of a pond. It is a less distinct brick-built path which leads up past rhododendrons to a stone wall, where you go right. Follow the wall to the left, and then right, to return to the car park at the start.

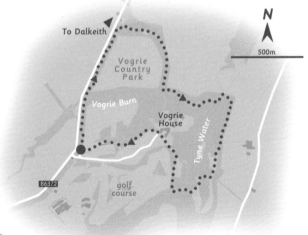

19

Dalkeith Country Park

Distance **6km** Time **2 hours**
Terrain **surfaced and unsurfaced
paths and tracks** Map **OS Explorer
350** Access **buses from Joppa to
Dalkeith Corn Exchange, 900m
from the start of the walk; small
entry fee to the estate**

**Dalkeith Country Park has
long been a popular family
destination with an adventure
playground, upmarket eateries
and shops, the restoration of
wonderful historic features
and easy-to-follow trails.**

The walk begins at the Orangerie,
built in the 1830s by William Burn,
who also added the clocktower and
belfry to the estate's nearby coach-
houses. Originally used to grow exotic
fruit for the Duke of Buccleuch, this
exquisite conservatory with its Doric
columns and Jacobean detailing is a
symbol of the wealth and status the
estate has enjoyed in the 300 years it
has been in the Buccleuch family.

Dalkeith Palace, the estate's stately
home, was completed in 1711 by

James Smith, architect of the since-
demolished Hamilton Palace, who
modelled the building on William of
Orange's Het Loo Palace in the
Netherlands. Described as 'the
grandest of all early classical houses
in Lothian', it hosted Bonnie Prince
Charlie in 1745, the year of the
Jacobite Rebellion. It was also chosen
ahead of the Palace of Holyroodhouse
as a place to stay by King George IV
on his visit to Edinburgh in 1822.

The Palace is now let to the
University of Wisconsin for a study
abroad programme which means it is
not open to the public. More than
1000 acres of the estate can,
however, still be explored.

Head northeast from the Orangerie,
over the stone Laundry Bridge,
designed by William Adam in around
1740, and carry straight on along a
driveway which leads across farmland.
Once across a footbridge over the
A68, go left at two junctions to reach
Smeaton Bridge. Cross this and follow
the driveway to the right.

On reaching a large fork go left, then

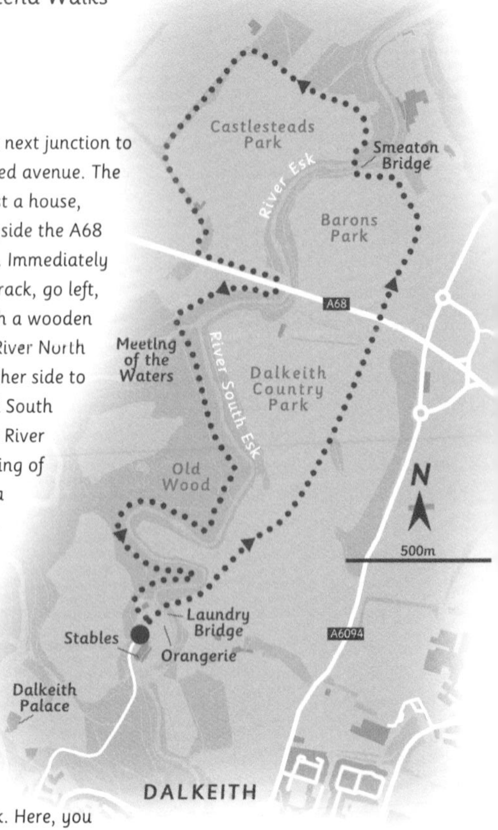

turn left again at the next junction to walk along a tree-lined avenue. The track swings left, past a house, before running alongside the A68 and passing under it. Immediately before a fork in the track, go left, down a path to reach a wooden footbridge over the River North Esk. Go left on the other side to where the North and South Esk meet to form the River Esk. The actual Meeting of the Waters is down a little path to the left.

Follow the main path to the right, along the River South Esk. Ignore turnings on the right until the path swings away from the river and becomes more of a grass track. Here, you can detour to the right to a small idyllic pond fringed by trees.

Where the main grass track ends at a gate, take the path on the left.

At a fork go left to descend to the bottom of a steep slope, then right to take the riverside path back to Laundry Bridge.

Map labels: Castlesteads Park, Smeaton Bridge, River Esk, Barons Park, A68, Meeting of the Waters, River South Esk, Dalkeith Country Park, Old Wood, N, 500m, Laundry Bridge, Stables, Orangerie, A6094, Dalkeith Palace, DALKEITH

20

Newhailes

Distance **2.5km** Time **1 hour**
Terrain **paths, muddy in places,
access road** Map **OS Explorer 350**
Access **buses from Edinburgh to
Newhailes**

**Newhailes, in the care of the
National Trust for Scotland, is
often bypassed as visitors head
to coast or city. This Palladian
masterpiece is well worth a visit,
however. Surrounded by pleasure
grounds with follies and old
walkways, it is also a habitat for
tawny owls and butterflies, with
views out to the Firth of Forth.**

Go through the main gates off the
roundabout on Newhailes Road: the
car park is just inside the gates on the
left. Walk down the drive to a junction
where you go left to walk on the
right-hand side of the old stable block.
A path goes right from the side of the
stable block before veering left in front
of the main house, built in 1686 as the
family home of architect James Smith,
a quarter of a century before he
designed Dalkeith Palace. It was later
home to the Dalrymples, who built the
lavish additions and a vast library
whose contents, now held at the
National Library of Scotland, are
regarded as the most important
contemporary surviving collection
from the Scottish Enlightenment era.
Leading literary figure Dr Samuel
Johnson described the library at the
time 'as the most learned room in
Europe' and it became a hub for
Enlightenment writers and thinkers,
including James Boswell, David Hume
and Johnson himself.

At a junction of paths go right and
pass through a metal gate. After
entering woodland, you can detour
right to the Earl of Stair Monument,
built to commemorate the 2nd Earl
who fought as second in command to
George II at Dettingen in 1743. Part of
the War of the Austrian Succession, it
was the last battle attended by a
British King. Otherwise continue to a
shell grotto, part of the Dalrymples'
designed landscape, dating back to
the mid-1700s and decorated with
pieces of shell, glass and semi-precious

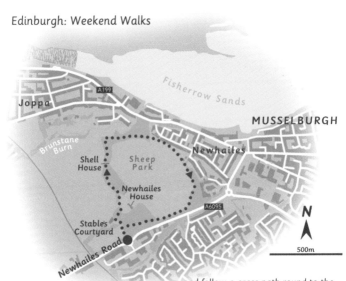

stones, with a black-and-white tiled floor and a pool to the front.

Ignore another turning up to the right further on and continue down the side of a burn which once formed the estate's water gardens. The path leads to the ruins of a summerhouse (the Tea House).

Turn right, then keep right to reach the edge of a field where you go left to reach the end of a brick wall. This was once the Ladies' Walk, an elevated structure which maximised the views.

Go left in front of a wooden gate and follow a grass path round to the right, from where you can look over to Musselburgh and the Firth of Forth. The main house can be seen to the right, across a vast field known as Sheep Park. A grass track which leads up to formal lawns was once the main entrance – go straight ahead rather than along this.

The path aims for a corner of Sheep Park, where you go right. At the second corner of the field go straight ahead at a junction of paths to walk through woodland and reach the drive. Turn left to return to Newhailes Road.

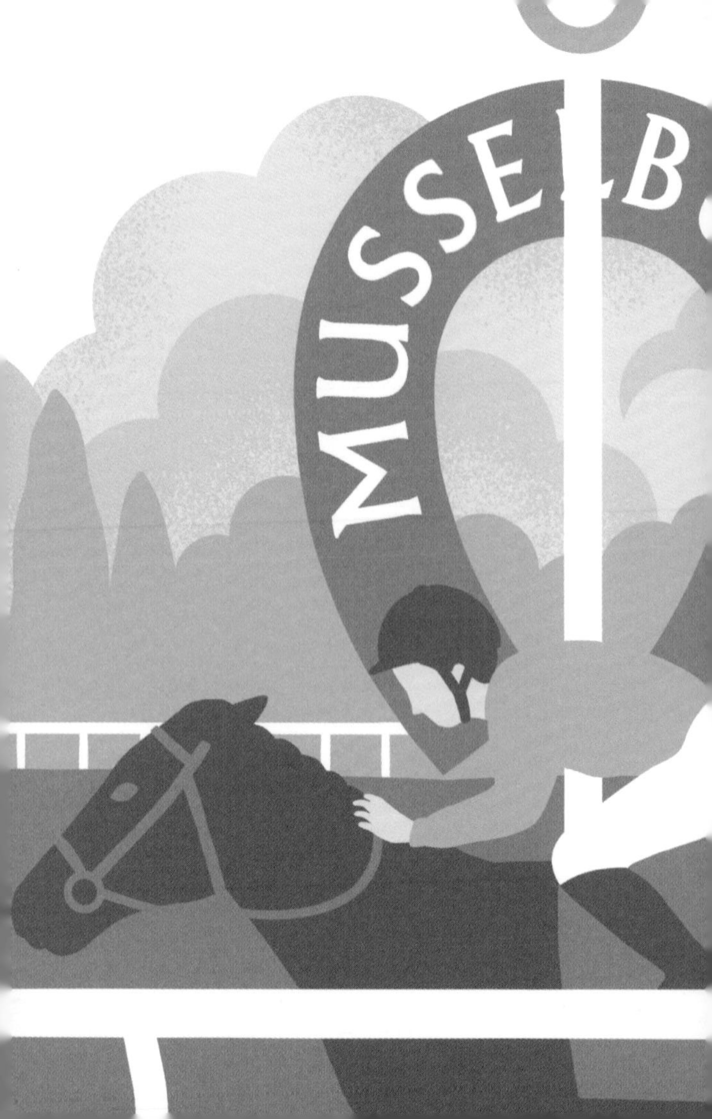
MUSSELB

21

Musselburgh and Levenhall Links

Distance **8km** Time **2 hours 15**
Terrain **surfaced and unsurfaced
paths and tracks, pavements**
Map **OS Explorer 350**
Access **buses from Edinburgh to
Fisherrow, Musselburgh**

**Musselburgh has a proud fishing
tradition and the promenade
from Fisherrow to the mouth of
the River Esk pays homage to
this with its statues and
memorials above the strand of
beach. Beyond this is a remnant
of a more recent industrial past;
ash lagoons which once held
waste from the former Cockenzie
Power Station are now a nature
reserve and a haven for birdlife.**

Start at the 18th-century Fisherrow
Harbour where clinking yachts and
dinghies have replaced the traditional
fishing boats that once plied the
coastal waters off the Lothians for
herring and white fish. Fisherrow was
rejected in favour of Dunbar by Oliver

Cromwell in his search for a port
during his 1650 campaign in Scotland
and remained a fishing harbour, with
28 craft and 140 fishermen at its peak
in the 1830s. Close to here is the site
of a Roman harbour which served a
fort at the nearby village of Inveresk.

Facing the harbour, go right to
follow the promenade above
Fisherrow Sands (or, if you prefer, the
beach). Ignore turnings to the right as
you take a wide surfaced path past
playing fields and houses until you
emerge at the River Esk near the point
where it flows into the Firth of Forth.

Follow the river upstream to cross it
by a pedestrian bridge. Head back
downstream, following a road all the
way to an Army Cadet Force building,
which you pass on your left. Now on
a path, keep by the river to soon
swing round to the right along the
shores of the Firth of Forth. To your
right are the former ash lagoons, now
a roost for wading and seabirds.

Ignore a track on the right but 350m

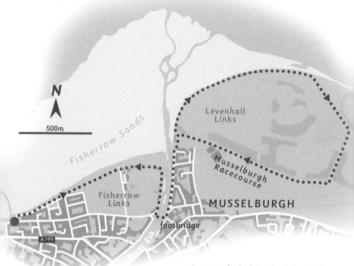

later, go right onto a path which starts next to a sign for a bird reserve – this is a place to look for eiders, terns and great crested grebes, as well as seals in the firth. Walk left of an ash lagoon, then follow a car park to a track.

Go right where the track bends left to follow a path running next to Musselburgh Racecourse, home to the 'Edinburgh Races' when they moved from Leith Sands in 1816. In the middle of the racecourse is the nine-hole Musselburgh Links Old Golf

Course which dates back to 1672 (almost 150 years before the horses arrived) and is the oldest in the world still being played. It was the venue of six Open Championships between 1874 and 1889.

As the racecourse curves away to the left carry straight on, following a track to the right of some stables and a maintenance yard. Pass the BMX cycle track to reach the Army Cadet Force hut passed earlier and go left to retrace your steps along the river and back to Fisherrow Harbour.

22

Carberry Hill

Distance **4km** Time **1 hour 15**
Terrain **paths (muddy in places)**
and tracks Map **OS Explorer 351**
Access **buses from Musselburgh to**
Whitecraig, 2.5km from the start

The sound of birdsong and the
sight of fields rolling down to
the Firth of Forth are a pleasant
backdrop to any walk, yet
Carberry Hill was also the scene
of one of the seismic moments
in Scotland's history.

A commemorative stone on Queen
Mary's Mount marks the spot where,
in June 1567, Mary, Queen of Scots
surrendered to the Confederate Lords,
but only after she had secured the
escape of her unpopular husband
James Hepburn, Earl of Bothwell, who
was suspected of involvement in the
murder of Mary's second husband,
Lord Darnley. The following month
Mary was forced to abdicate and
although she initially escaped
imprisonment she was executed by
Queen Elizabeth I of England 20 years
later. As well as hastening her own

end, Mary's efforts to secure safe
passage for Bothwell were ultimately
unsuccessful: he died in 1578 after
spending more than a decade going
insane, cruelly chained to a pillar in
a Danish castle dungeon.

To begin the walk, go up Springfield
Steading, 300m northwest of
Crossgatehall, off the A6124. At the
top of a track go right to cross a car
park and take a track at the other
end. Ignore a path immediately on the
left to take another path on the left
after 100m. This climbs through mixed
woodland, crossing a track higher up.
At a junction go left, then cross over
another path further up.

Join a track on the left and continue
uphill to a fork, where you go right.
Ignore turnings on either side and
follow the narrow path up and to the
right to reach Queen Mary's Mount.
It is hard to keep sight of the fact that
such an important event took place
here, such is the understated nature of
the commemorative stone, next to a
field with a view over farmland to the
Firth of Forth. An Iron Age hillfort

85

once stood here, though there is little evidence of it now.

On this walk you are also following in the footsteps of Queen Elizabeth II who often visited the Carberry Tower estate as a child when the Queen Mother's sister, Lady Margaret Elphinstone, lived here.

Retrace your steps for 50m and take the second path on the right. At the next two junctions go right to continue downhill. The path goes straight down and over a mountain bike trail. Ignore turnings until the gradient eases and you reach a wider path where you go left. Bear right at a fence with a large field on the other side. The path leads you through a wooden gate on the left to then follow an avenue of redwoods. At the end of this go through another gate and turn left onto a track. The track runs by a field to the junction near the earlier car park. Go right here to return to the start.

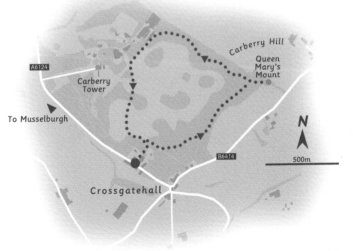

23

Seton Collegiate Church and Sands

Distance 6km **Time** 2 hours
Terrain surfaced and unsurfaced
paths, pavement **Map** OS Explorer
351 **Access** buses from Edinburgh
stop near Seton East Farm, 500m
from the start

**Seton Collegiate Church stands
sheltered by trees above a lovely
stretch of sandy coastline on the
Firth of Forth. Damaged during
the 'Rough Wooing' of the
1540s, put out of use by the 1560
Reformation and ransacked after
the 1715 Jacobite Rising, its
blissfully peaceful setting belies
its turbulent past.**

There has been a church here since
the 1100s but it had collegiate status
from the 1490s after, like many
wealthy landowners of the day, the
1st Lord Seton established a college
of priests to pray for his family.

During the 'Rough Wooing' by
Henry VIII, a 'war' designed to enforce
the marriage alliance between the
infant Mary, Queen of Scots and
Edward, English heir apparent, both
the Collegiate Church and the Seton
residence of Seton Palace were left
badly damaged. Though the church
was repaired, in fewer than 20 years
collegiate life was to be brought to a
close as the Reformation of 1560
swept across Scotland. The estate was
forfeited and the church damaged
again after the Jacobite Rising of
1715, the Setons having been devout
supporters of the exiled James Edward
Stuart. The Setons' glorious
Renaissance Palace that had been
used to entertain Mary, Queen of
Scots, among many others, fell into
disrepair and was demolished in
1789 to make way for Seton Castle,
designed by Robert Adam.

Leave the A198 on a path to the left
of the car park for the church. Walk
through woodland to a track, where
you go right to reach the church –
open in summer (entry fee).

Beyond the church, stay on the main

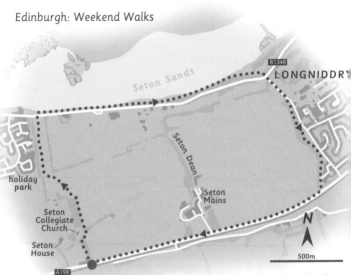

path which goes left, then drops to the
right. After emerging from the woods
into a large field follow the path down
to the left. At dusk and dawn this is a
great place to spot owls hunting for
prey. Keep left to reach the corner of
the field and pass through a gap in a
wooden fence before going right.
A path leads down to the B1348
which runs along the Firth of Forth.

Cross the road and turn right to
follow the coast for 1.6km with views
to Fife. If you choose to drop down

and walk along the sands rather than
the pavement, leave the beach at the
second of two burns (Canty Burn) and
head up to a car park, which you
leave by a path to the right.

Re-cross the B1348 to take a path
next to a minor road through a golf
course. Ignore turns to either side
after going through a kissing gate to
follow the burn up Longniddry Dean.

After a series of footbridges you
pass three sets of steps on the left
before meeting the A198. Go right
here to follow the pavement for 1.5km
to the start.

Gosford Estate

Distance **5km** Time **2 hours**
Terrain **surfaced and unsurfaced
paths and tracks**
Map **OS Explorer 351** Access **buses
from Edinburgh to the west side of
Aberlady, 250m from the start**

**Gosford House, home to the Earl
of Wemyss and March, is one of
the grandest stately homes in
Britain. As you peer through
trees and across lawns you
would be forgiven for expecting
to see characters from a period
drama. The grounds are just as
spectacular and can be enjoyed
on designated paths.**

The house was based on a design by
celebrated neoclassical architect
Robert Adam, who died in 1792, eight
years before Gosford was completed.
Though much altered after his death,
it is still regarded as one of his
masterpieces. Be aware that it is a
private residence, so keep to the paths.

Start at a car park at the top of a
track by the A198 to the west of
Aberlady. Walk down the track to
reach the Gosford Bothy farm shop,
where you can buy a £1 day permit to
walk around the grounds. (Note that
the gates close at 5pm for cars, but
the grounds are still open for walkers.)

Go right in front of the shop and
walk across a car park, going left at
the far side in front of a walled
garden. A track leads through a gate
and along the wall of the garden,
turning right at the end. Ignore two
tracks on the left, then at a junction
go left to walk in front of the
mausoleum where the body of the
7th Earl of Wemyss is interred, along
with the ashes of mathematician
Dr Norman Routledge who taught
the 13th Earl and died in 2013.

Follow the track down from the
mausoleum and take a grass path on
the left, just before a low stone bridge.
Keep right to walk over a footbridge
and through a wooden gate before
reaching the ornate Ice House. Go
right in front of this to reach a lily
pond, then go left to join a grass path
on the edge of a large ornamental
pond. Go left and walk round the

91

pond, ignoring a turning on the right. The ponds were designed by James Ramsay in the 1790s to encircle the romantic pleasure ground, making it very nearly an island. Another fine building, the Curling House, is passed before the path leads behind a grand boathouse, which was also used for bathing. Keep following the path up the other side of the pond until 20m after a wide grass track has crossed the water. Go left into woodland here, and bear right

past an information board. After 150m, look for a wooden footbridge on the left and cross over it to follow a path to a track, where you go left.

Keeping to the track, ignore a path on the left, which leads back to the boathouse, to emerge at a junction. Take a track on the left and follow it all the way to the edge of the walled garden. Go right here to retrace your steps to the start.

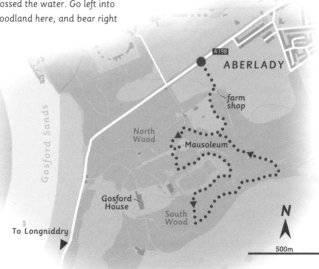

Aberlady Bay and Gullane Point

Distance **6.5km** Time **2 hours 15**
Terrain **surfaced and unsurfaced
paths and tracks, sandy beach**
Map **OS Explorer 351**
Access **buses from Edinburgh to
the east edge of Aberlady, 800m
from the start**

**Aberlady Bay became Britain's
first Local Nature Reserve in
1952, with a range of plants,
animals and geology found
here. The saltmarsh, rocky
outcrops and long sandy beach
make it a great place for a
walk. Please note, dogs are
not allowed as they are a risk
to ground-nesting birds.**

Look out for skylarks, lapwings
and even ospreys, and for prime
birdwatching leave your visit until
autumn when around 30,000 pink-
footed geese arrive from Iceland. Dogs
are banned but one prevalent four-
legged animal is roe deer, best seen at
sunset or on a quiet winter's day.

The walk begins at a car park by the
A198 which lies 800m from the east
edge of Aberlady. Cross a long
wooden footbridge over the Peffer
Burn, following a path to the left on
the other side and then going through
a tunnel of sea buckthorn. This plant
may look pretty, and it is native, but
major efforts are made to stop it
spreading and choking out other
plants. Some claim the bitter berries
are a 'super fruit', however.

The path then twists through the
thorny bushes before passing Marl
Loch. An obvious path continues
along marshy grassland to the
twittering of hundreds of birds to
reach a track. Go left and follow the
track for 400m where you go right at
a footpath sign. A grass path skirts
one of the hallowed greens of Gullane
Golf Club, then continues up to a
track, where you go left.

Follow the track uphill in a straight
line to a junction, where you go left
down a path signed for Gullane Point.

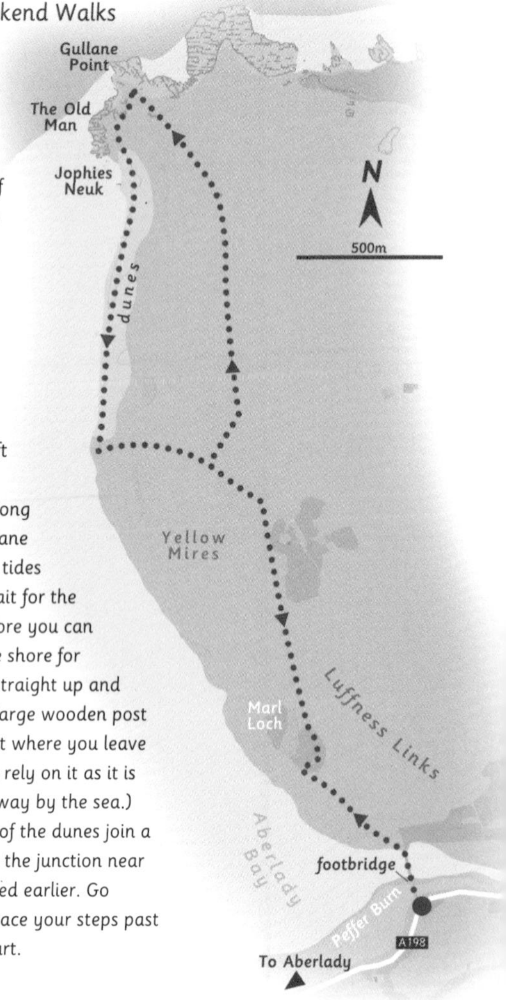

Edinburgh: Weekend Walks

Go left at a fork, then pass dunes to reach the point itself with rocky outcrops plunging into the Firth of Forth – the views stretch from Arthur's Seat and the Forth bridges in the west to Gullane Bay in the east.

The route turns left 30m before Gullane Point, down to the long sandy beach of Gullane Sands. At very high tides you may have to wait for the water to recede before you can carry on. Follow the shore for 750m, then go left straight up and over the dunes. (A large wooden post often marks the spot where you leave the beach but don't rely on it as it is regularly washed away by the sea.)

On the other side of the dunes join a path which leads to the junction near the golf green, passed earlier. Go straight on and retrace your steps past Marl Loch to the start.

Gullane Point

The Old Man

Jophies Neuk

dunes

N

500m

Yellow Mires

Luffness Links

Marl Loch

Aberlady Bay

footbridge

Peffer Burn

A198

To Aberlady